CREDIT PROTECTION BLUEPRINT

A STEP-BY-STEP PLAN TO FREEZE YOUR CREDIT, STOP FRAUD, AND PROTECT YOUR SCORE BEFORE UNEXPECTED ISSUES UNDO YOUR PROGRESS

ROMITO MONEYGREEN

INT COM INTERNATIONAL

CONTENTS

INTRODUCTION

WHY CREDIT PROTECTION MATTERS *AFTER* YOU FIX AND PAY DOWN DEBT

Fixing your credit and paying down debt feels like the finish line.

For many people, it's actually the **most vulnerable moment**.

Once balances drop and scores improve, your credit becomes more valuable—and therefore more exposed. Fewer negative items, cleaner reports, and newly available credit create conditions where **small problems cause bigger damage** than before.

That's the hidden risk most people never see coming.

THE RISK THAT APPEARS ONCE CREDIT IMPROVES

When your credit is damaged, lenders expect instability.

When your credit improves, the system assumes stability.

That's when:

- unauthorized accounts stand out more sharply
- reporting errors have greater impact

- delayed responses cost more points
- fraud causes faster, more noticeable drops

Ironically, the better your credit becomes, the **less margin for error** you have.

WHY MOST SCORE DROPS HAPPEN AFTER PROGRESS

Many people believe credit score drops happen because of missed payments or bad behavior.

Often, they happen because of:

- outdated information re-reporting
- new accounts you didn't open
- incorrect balances or limits
- delayed detection of small issues

The problem isn't effort.

It's **lack of early defense**.

By the time most people notice something is wrong, damage is already done.

WHAT CREDIT PROTECTION REALLY MEANS (AND WHAT IT DOESN'T)

Credit protection is not:

- obsessively checking your score
- paying for expensive monitoring services
- living in fear of identity theft

Real credit protection is:

- limiting unauthorized access
- detecting issues early
- responding calmly and correctly
- protecting progress without constant attention

It's about systems—not surveillance.

WHO THIS BOOK IS FOR (AND WHO IT ISN'T)

This book is for you if:

- you've improved your credit or are actively doing so
- you want to protect progress without paranoia
- you value preparation over reaction

This book is **not** for:

- people looking for shortcuts or guarantees
- those unwilling to follow simple procedures
- anyone seeking total elimination of risk

Protection reduces risk—it doesn't pretend to erase it.

HOW TO USE THIS BOOK WITHOUT FEAR OR OBSESSION

Read this book as a **playbook**, not a warning.

Follow the steps in order.

Use the checklists when needed.

Review monthly, not daily.

Credit protection should feel calm, boring, and effective.

When systems are in place, anxiety disappears—and control takes its place.

That's what this book is here to help you build.

PART I — UNDERSTANDING THE REAL RISKS

CHAPTER 1
HOW CREDIT GETS DAMAGED WITHOUT WARNING

Most serious credit problems don't start with a missed payment.

They start quietly—often without any action on your part.

That's what makes them dangerous.

This chapter explains **how credit damage actually happens after progress**, and why waiting to "see if something goes wrong" is not a neutral choice.

REPORTING ERRORS VS. FRAUD: TWO DIFFERENT THREATS

Credit damage usually comes from one of two sources:

Reporting errors or **fraud**.

They are often confused—but they behave very differently.

Reporting errors include:

- incorrect balances or limits
- accounts reported as late when they weren't
- outdated information reappearing
- duplicated or misclassified accounts

These errors are common, usually unintentional, and often slow to surface.

They don't feel urgent—until they affect your score.

Fraud, on the other hand, is intentional:

- accounts opened without your knowledge
- unauthorized inquiries
- misuse of personal information

Fraud moves faster and causes sharper damage.

Both can hurt your score.

Both require different responses.

And neither announces itself clearly.

UNAUTHORIZED ACCOUNTS: THE SILENT CREDIT THREAT

Unauthorized accounts rarely trigger immediate alarms.

Often, they:

- appear as small credit lines
- remain inactive for weeks
- go unnoticed until reporting updates

By the time you discover them, your score may already be affected.

This is why people say:

"My score dropped and I don't know why."

The account wasn't obvious.

The damage wasn't immediate.

But the impact was real.

DATA BREACHES AND DELAYED DETECTION

You don't need to be careless to be exposed.

Large data breaches happen regularly—and your information may already be compromised without your knowledge.

The danger isn't the breach itself.

It's **delay**.

When detection is slow:

- unauthorized activity blends into normal reporting
- response windows are missed
- correction takes longer

Credit systems reward speed.

Delay multiplies damage.

WHY "DOING NOTHING" IS STILL A RISK

Many people believe that if they don't touch their credit, nothing can go wrong.

That's not protection.

That's exposure.

Doing nothing means:

- errors persist longer
- fraud goes unnoticed
- small issues become large ones

Credit protection isn't about constant action.

It's about **intentional inaction with safeguards in place**.

Locks.

Checks.

Response plans.

Without them, inaction becomes a risk.

Credit damage after progress is rarely dramatic.

It's quiet, incremental, and easy to miss.

That's why protection must come **before** problems appear—not after.

In the next chapter, you'll learn exactly **what to monitor and what to ignore**, so protection stays calm, efficient, and effective.

CHAPTER 2
CREDIT REPORTS: WHAT TO MONITOR (AND WHAT TO IGNORE)

One of the fastest ways to turn credit protection into anxiety is trying to monitor **everything**.

Credit reports contain a lot of information—but only a **small portion of it actually matters** for protecting your score. The rest is noise.

This chapter shows you how to focus on the signals that matter and ignore the distractions that don't.

WHAT ACTUALLY MATTERS ON A CREDIT REPORT

When your goal is protection—not repair—you're looking for **changes**, not perfection.

These are the items that deserve your attention:

- **New accounts you don't recognize**

Any account you didn't open yourself is a red flag and requires immediate action.

- **New hard inquiries**

Especially those not tied to an application you made.

- **Balance or limit changes on existing accounts**

Incorrect balances or reduced limits can raise utilization and hurt your score quickly.

- **Account status changes**

Open → closed, current → delinquent, or any unexpected reclassification.

- **Personal information changes**

New addresses, employers, or name variations you didn't provide can signal fraud or data misuse.

These items directly affect risk, utilization, or identity integrity.

They're what credit protection is designed to catch early.

WHAT DOESN'T REQUIRE YOUR ATTENTION

Many report details look alarming but are usually harmless.

You generally do **not** need to stress about:

- minor score fluctuations
- old, accurate accounts already paid or closed
- small month-to-month balance changes
- harmless soft inquiries
- variations between different scoring models

Trying to "fix" these often creates unnecessary disputes or emotional decisions that cause more harm than good.

Protection is about restraint as much as action.

HOW OFTEN TO CHECK—AND WHY OVERCHECKING BACKFIRES

Checking too often creates three problems:

1. **False urgency** — normal updates look like threats
2. **Decision fatigue** — you react instead of evaluate
3. **Anxiety without benefit** — because reports don't update daily

A healthy protection rhythm looks like this:

- **Monthly check:** scan for new accounts, inquiries, or errors
- **Quarterly deep review:** confirm everything still makes sense
- **Immediate check:** only if you receive a real alert or notice

Anything more frequent doesn't improve outcomes—it just increases stress.

Credit protection isn't about constant vigilance.

It's about **focused awareness.**

When you know what to watch—and what to ignore—you stay calm, responsive, and in control.

In the next chapter, you'll learn the most powerful protection tool available:

freezing your credit the right way.

PART II — FREEZE & PREVENT

CHAPTER 3
CREDIT FREEZE EXPLAINED (WITHOUT CONFUSION)

Few credit tools are as powerful—and as misunderstood—as the credit freeze.

Some people avoid it because they think it's extreme.

Others activate it incorrectly and lock themselves into frustration.

This chapter explains credit freezes **clearly, calmly, and correctly**, so you can use them as protection—not punishment.

CREDIT FREEZE VS. FRAUD ALERT VS. CREDIT LOCK

These three tools are often lumped together, but they are **not the same**.

Credit Freeze

A credit freeze completely restricts access to your credit file.

No new accounts can be opened unless you temporarily lift or remove the freeze.

- Free by law
- Strongest form of protection
- Requires action to unlock

Fraud Alert

A fraud alert places a note on your file asking lenders to verify identity.

- Free
- Weaker protection
- Relies on human follow-through

Fraud alerts don't stop access—they request caution.

Credit Lock

A credit lock functions like a freeze but is usually tied to a paid monitoring service.

- Often marketed aggressively
- Not legally stronger than a freeze
- Can be removed if the service is canceled

In short:

- **Freeze = control**
- **Alert = request**
- **Lock = paid convenience**

For long-term protection, the freeze is the foundation.

WHEN A CREDIT FREEZE MAKES SENSE

A credit freeze is not only for people who have been victims of fraud.

It makes sense if:

- your credit is clean or improving
- you don't plan to apply for credit frequently
- you want to eliminate unauthorized access entirely
- you prefer prevention over reaction

Freezing your credit doesn't harm your score.

It doesn't affect existing accounts.

It simply closes the door to new risk.

For many people, it's the single most effective protection step they'll ever take.

COMMON MYTHS AND COSTLY MISTAKES

Let's clear up the most common misconceptions.

Myth: "A freeze will hurt my credit score."

Reality: It has zero impact on your score.

Myth: "I'll never be able to open credit again."

Reality: Freezes can be lifted temporarily, often in minutes.

Myth: "Monitoring is enough."

Reality: Monitoring tells you *after* something happens. Freezes stop it from happening.

Mistake: Forgetting where or how to lift a freeze

Fix: Keep credentials secure and document your process.

Mistake: Freezing one bureau but not all

Fix: Protection only works when applied consistently.

The Right Perspective

A credit freeze isn't paranoia.

It's **permission-based access**.

You decide when credit is available—and when it isn't.

In the next chapter, you'll learn exactly how to freeze and unfreeze your credit safely, without stress or mistakes.

DECISION FRAME — NEW INQUIRY APPEARS

Situation:

A new inquiry shows up on your credit report.

Question:

Do I recognize this inquiry?

□ **YES → Do this:**

- Monitor only
- Confirm it aligns with a recent application
- Take no further action

□ **NO → Do this:**

- Freeze credit immediately (if not already frozen)
- Contact the bureau and lender
- File a **defensive dispute**

If you're unsure:

Wait 24–48 hours and verify before acting.

Unknown inquiries require action. Known ones require patience.

CHAPTER 4
HOW TO FREEZE AND UNFREEZE YOUR CREDIT SAFELY

A credit freeze is only effective if you can **control it confidently**.

Done right, it's simple, reversible, and stress-free.

Done wrong, it can feel like you locked the door and lost the key.

This chapter walks you through the process step by step—so protection never turns into frustration.

THE STEP-BY-STEP FREEZE PROCESS

Freezing your credit is a **bureau-by-bureau action**. To be fully protected, you must complete the process with **all three** credit bureaus.

Follow this order:

1. Create a secure account with each bureau

Use a strong, unique password and a secure email address you check regularly.

2. Verify your identity

This may include knowledge-based questions or document verification. Take your time—accuracy matters.

3. Activate the freeze

Once confirmed, your credit file becomes inaccessible to new applications.

4. Record your access details

Save usernames, passwords, and recovery options in a secure location (password manager or written backup).

That's it.

No fees. No score impact. No changes to existing accounts.

TEMPORARY LIFTS AND UNFREEZES (THE RIGHT WAY)

Freezes are not permanent barriers—they're **controlled gates**.

You have three options when you need access:

- **Temporary lift** for a specific time window
- **Temporary lift** for a specific creditor
- **Full removal** (not recommended unless necessary)

Best **practice**:

- Lift the freeze **only for the shortest time needed**
- Schedule the lift **before** applying
- Re-freeze immediately after approval

Most lifts take minutes—not days—when done online.

HOW TO AVOID LOCKING YOURSELF OUT

The most common problems aren't technical—they're organizational.

Avoid these mistakes:

- Using different emails and forgetting which is tied to which bureau
- Losing recovery questions or backup codes
- Waiting until the last minute to lift a freeze

- Freezing without documenting the process

Simple safeguards:

- Keep a single "Credit Protection" note with all access details
- Set calendar reminders for temporary lifts
- Test a lift once to understand the flow before you actually need it

A credit freeze is not a restriction—it's **selective access**.

When you control the door, you control the risk.

In the next chapter, you'll strengthen that control by learning how to reduce fraud risk **before** your information is ever misused.

CREDIT FREEZE CHECKLIST

A clear, step-by-step checklist to:

- freeze your credit correctly at all bureaus
- confirm protection is fully active
- avoid common setup mistakes

This ensures your strongest defense is in place—and stays there.

(Download in Bonus Section)

DECISION FRAME — APPLYING FOR CREDIT WHILE FROZEN

Situation:

You're applying for new credit.

Question:

Do I need permanent access?

□ **NO → Do this:**

- Temporarily lift freeze for lender or time window
- Re-freeze after approval

☐ **YES → Do this:**

- Remove freeze only if absolutely necessary
- Reinstate protection immediately after

Never leave access open longer than necessary.

CHAPTER 5
PREVENTING FRAUD BEFORE IT STARTS

The best response to fraud is never needing one.

Most credit problems don't happen because someone is careless.

They happen because **small, preventable weak points** go unnoticed.

This chapter focuses on reducing risk *before* anything goes wrong—quietly, consistently, and without fear.

PROTECTING YOUR PERSONAL DATA

Your credit is only as secure as the information tied to it.

High-risk data includes:

- Social Security number
- date of birth
- full legal name
- current and past addresses

You don't need to hide these details from the world—but you should **control where they live**.

Smart data protection habits:

- avoid storing sensitive documents in email inboxes
- shred physical paperwork you no longer need
- limit how often you share personal information "just in case"
- question requests that feel unnecessary or rushed

Less exposure means fewer opportunities for misuse.

ACCOUNT ACCESS HYGIENE

Fraud doesn't always start with identity theft.

Often, it starts with **account access**.

Clean access habits include:

- removing saved cards from online stores
- reviewing connected devices and sessions periodically
- logging out of financial accounts on shared or public devices
- avoiding financial actions on unsecured Wi-Fi networks

Access should be intentional—not automatic.

EMAIL, PASSWORDS, AND COMMON WEAK POINTS

Email is the gateway to almost everything.

If someone controls your email, they can:

- reset passwords
- approve logins
- intercept alerts

Strengthen this first:

- use a strong, unique password for your primary email
- enable two-factor authentication
- avoid reusing email passwords anywhere else

For financial accounts:

- never reuse passwords
- prioritize password managers over memory
- update passwords after major breaches—not constantly

Security works best when it's **structured**, not reactive.

HABITS THAT QUIETLY REDUCE RISK

You don't need extreme measures to stay protected.

Low-effort, high-impact habits:

- review account alerts once per week
- pause before responding to urgent messages
- verify sources before clicking links
- keep credit freezes active when not applying

These habits don't feel dramatic—but they work.

Fraud prevention isn't about paranoia.

It's about **reducing exposure and increasing friction**.

When access is limited and habits are clean,

most threats never reach your credit in the first place.

In the next chapter, you'll learn how to recognize early warning signs—so small issues never become big ones.

DECISION FRAME — DATA BREACH NOTIFICATION

Situation:

You receive a data breach email.

Question:

Is my credit currently frozen?

□ **YES → Do this:**

- Secure email and passwords
- Increase monitoring temporarily

□ **NO → Do this:**

- Freeze credit immediately
- Document breach date

Do NOT:

- panic
- dispute anything
- apply for credit

Breach ≠ fraud. Preparation beats reaction.

PART III — REAL-LIFE CREDIT PROTECTION SCENARIOS

CHAPTER 6
SCENARIO 1 — "MY SCORE DROPPED 40 POINTS OVERNIGHT"

This section exists for one reason:

real credit problems don't show up as theory.

They show up as situations.

Most people don't fail because they don't know *what* to do.

They fail because, in the moment, they don't know **which rule applies right now**.

These scenarios bridge that gap.

Each one is written to help you recognize the situation, stay calm, and apply the correct response—without panic or overreaction.

SCENARIO 1 — "MY SCORE DROPPED 40 POINTS OVERNIGHT"

Few things trigger panic faster than this.

You open an app.

You see the number.

And your first thought is usually:

"What did I mess up?"

In many cases, the answer is: **nothing.**

WHAT THIS SCENARIO USUALLY LOOKS LIKE

- Your credit score drops 30–50 points suddenly
- You didn't miss a payment
- You didn't apply for new credit
- You didn't increase spending significantly

The drop feels unexplained—and that's what makes it dangerous.

THE MOST COMMON CAUSES

A sudden drop like this is usually caused by one of three things:

1. A balance reported before your timing strategy took effect

One card reports high utilization for a single cycle.

2. A limit change or reporting update

Credit limits sometimes change without notice, affecting utilization.

3. Delayed reporting from a previous cycle

The system catches up before your actions are reflected.

Notice what's missing here:

reckless behavior.

WHAT *NOT* TO DO FIRST

This is where most people make things worse.

Do **not**:

- dispute anything immediately
- unfreeze or refreeze impulsively
- apply for credit "to test it"

- panic-adjust your entire strategy

Overreaction creates new problems.

THE CORRECT RESPONSE (STEP-BY-STEP)

1. Pause for 24–48 hours

Many drops correct themselves once updated balances report.

2. Check high-impact cards only

Look for utilization spikes or reporting timing issues.

3. Confirm no new accounts or inquiries

If none exist, fraud is unlikely.

4. Stay the course unless new information appears

This is usually a reporting delay, not a failure.

WHY THIS SCENARIO FEELS WORSE THAN IT IS

When credit improves, volatility feels scarier—even when the impact is temporary.

The key skill here is **discernment**, not action.

Most overnight drops resolve within one reporting cycle when:

- balances are controlled
- timing is correct
- no unauthorized activity exists

Not every score drop is a threat.

Some are simply **lagging indicators catching up**.

Protection doesn't mean reacting faster.

It means reacting **only when necessary**.

CHAPTER 7
SCENARIO 2 — "AN ACCOUNT I NEVER OPENED APPEARED"

This is the moment most people fear—but few are prepared for.

You review your credit report.

Everything looks normal... until it doesn't.

A new account appears.

You don't recognize the lender.

You're certain you didn't open it.

At this point, **speed matters—but panic hurts**.

WHAT THIS SCENARIO USUALLY LOOKS LIKE

- A new credit card, loan, or line of credit appears
- You have no memory of applying
- The balance may be $0—or already active
- Your score may not have dropped yet

This last point is important.

Damage often comes later, not immediately.

THE TWO POSSIBLE EXPLANATIONS

There are only two realistic possibilities:

1. Fraud

Someone used your information to open an account.

2. Clerical or reporting error

Rare, but possible—especially with similar names or SSN mismatches.

Both require action.

Neither requires panic.

WHAT NOT TO DO FIRST

Your instinct may be to:

- dispute immediately
- call multiple bureaus at once
- unfreeze and refreeze randomly

Resist that urge.

Disorganized action slows resolution and creates confusion in records.

THE CORRECT RESPONSE (STEP-BY-STEP)

1. Confirm the account details

Check the opening date, lender name, and account type.

2. Freeze your credit immediately

If not already frozen, stop further exposure now.

3. Contact the lender directly

Ask whether the account was opened online or in person and request fraud procedures.

4. Document everything

Dates, names, reference numbers—write it all down.

5. Dispute the account with the bureaus

Use a **defensive dispute**, not a broad correction.

WHY ACTING EARLY MATTERS

Unauthorized accounts:

- are easier to remove early
- cause less score damage when stopped quickly
- create fewer downstream complications

Waiting turns a clean correction into a long cleanup.

Credit protection isn't about assuming fraud everywhere.

It's about **recognizing when something truly doesn't belong**.

If you didn't open the account,

you don't negotiate with it—you remove it.

CHAPTER 8
SCENARIO 3 — "A DATA BREACH EMAIL—WHAT NOW?"

It starts with an email.

A company you recognize—or barely remember—announces a data breach.

Your information *may* have been exposed.

No confirmation.

No immediate damage.

Just uncertainty.

This is where most people either **overreact** or **do nothing**.

Both are mistakes.

WHAT THIS SCENARIO USUALLY LOOKS LIKE

- You receive a breach notification email
- The company confirms possible exposure of personal data
- There is no immediate credit impact
- Your accounts appear normal—for now

The danger here is **delay**, not immediacy.

WHAT A DATA BREACH DOES (AND DOESN'T) MEAN

A breach does **not** mean:

- your credit has already been damaged
- accounts were opened
- fraud is guaranteed

It does mean:

- your information may circulate
- risk increases over time
- exposure can surface weeks or months later

The threat is **latent**, not urgent—but real.

THE CORRECT RESPONSE (STEP-BY-STEP)

1. Freeze your credit (if not already frozen)

This neutralizes most downstream risk immediately.

2. Secure account access points

Update passwords on:

- email
- financial accounts
- password manager

3. Ignore "free monitoring" pressure

Monitoring is optional. Prevention is not.

4. Document the breach date and source

This matters if something appears later.

5. Increase monitoring frequency temporarily

Monthly → biweekly for 60–90 days.

WHY DOING NOTHING IS RISKY

Most breach-related fraud doesn't happen immediately.

It happens **later**, when attention fades.

Freezes and preparation work because they **outlast attention spans**.

You don't need to react dramatically.

You need to **close doors before anyone tries them**.

Prepared responses beat emotional ones—every time.

CHAPTER 9
SCENARIO 4 — "APPLYING FOR CREDIT WHILE FROZEN"

This scenario doesn't involve fraud.

It involves **planning failure**.

You're ready to apply for credit.

Everything is lined up.

Then the application stalls.

Your credit is frozen—and you forgot.

WHAT THIS SCENARIO USUALLY LOOKS LIKE

- Application is delayed or denied
- Lender can't access your credit report
- You scramble to remember where and how to lift the freeze

This is inconvenient—but completely avoidable.

WHY THIS HAPPENS

Freezes work so well that people forget they're there.

That's not a failure.

That's success—without preparation.

The Correct Way to Handle It

1. Pause the application

Do not submit multiple applications.

2. Lift the freeze temporarily

- Use a specific time window
- Or allow access to a specific creditor

3. Confirm access before resubmitting

A single confirmation prevents repeat delays.

4. Re-freeze immediately after approval

Protection resumes automatically.

WHAT NOT TO DO

- Don't remove freezes permanently
- Don't rush applications under pressure
- Don't leave access open longer than necessary

Temporary access preserves long-term protection.

Freezes don't block opportunity.

They require **coordination**.

When planned properly, they're invisible.

When forgotten, they're frustrating—but fixable.

CHAPTER 10
SCENARIO 5 — "DISPUTING VS. WAITING: THE RIGHT CALL"

Not every credit issue requires immediate action.

Sometimes the most protective move is **waiting**.

Knowing the difference separates calm protection from reactive damage.

WHAT THIS SCENARIO USUALLY LOOKS LIKE

- A small score change appears
- A balance updates unexpectedly
- A minor discrepancy catches your eye

Nothing is clearly wrong—but something feels off.

THE URGE TO DISPUTE EVERYTHING

Fear creates urgency.

People dispute because:

- they don't want things to get worse
- they want control
- they assume action is always safer

Often, it isn't.

WHEN TO DISPUTE IMMEDIATELY

Dispute when the issue is:

- unauthorized
- clearly incorrect
- new and unexpected
- likely to cause continued damage

These are **defensive disputes**.

WHEN WAITING IS THE SMARTER MOVE

Wait when:

- changes align with reporting cycles
- information is accurate
- resolution is already in progress

Waiting allows systems to self-correct.

THE PROTECTION LESSON

Protection isn't speed.

It's **judgment**.

Act when risk is real.

Wait when it isn't.

That discernment is what keeps your credit safe **without obsession**.

CLOSING THOUGHT FOR THIS SECTION

Real-life credit problems don't announce themselves.

But when you recognize the pattern,

you don't panic—you respond.

That's what turns knowledge into protection.

PART IV — DETECT & RESPOND EARLY

CHAPTER 11
EARLY WARNING SIGNS SOMETHING IS WRONG

Serious credit problems rarely arrive with a loud alarm.

They usually begin with **small signals**—easy to dismiss, easy to delay, and costly if ignored.

This chapter teaches you how to recognize those early signs **without overreacting**, so you can respond quickly *when it matters* and stay calm when it doesn't.

SMALL SIGNALS PEOPLE OFTEN IGNORE

The earliest warnings are subtle.

Common examples include:

- a balance that looks slightly higher than expected
- a notification you don't fully recognize
- a new address or name variation on your report
- a change you assume will "sort itself out"

Individually, these don't feel urgent.

Collectively, they're how most credit damage starts.

The mistake isn't missing a signal once.

It's **ignoring patterns**.

UNEXPECTED CREDIT SCORE CHANGES

Not every score change is a problem—but some are.

Normal fluctuations:

- small drops or gains (a few points)
- temporary changes around reporting cycles

Concerning changes:

- sharp drops without a clear reason
- repeated declines over consecutive cycles
- drops that don't align with your known activity

If you haven't increased balances, missed payments, or applied for credit, a meaningful drop deserves investigation—not panic, but attention.

NEW INQUIRIES AND ACCOUNT ACTIVITY

New activity is the most important warning sign.

Pay attention to:

- hard inquiries you didn't authorize
- accounts you don't recognize
- notifications from lenders you've never used

These signals usually mean **time matters**.

The faster you act:

- the easier correction becomes
- the less damage spreads
- the fewer steps recovery requires

Delay turns small problems into complex ones.

WHEN TO ACT—AND WHEN TO WAIT

Protection isn't about reacting to everything.

Act immediately when:

- a new account appears that you didn't open
- a hard inquiry shows up without explanation
- personal information changes unexpectedly

Wait and observe when:

- a small score change aligns with a reporting cycle
- balances fluctuate normally
- nothing new appears on your report

The goal is balance:

responsive, not reactive

THE KEY SKILL OF CREDIT PROTECTION

The most valuable protection skill isn't speed—it's **discernment**.

When you know what matters, you don't waste energy chasing noise.

You save it for the moments that truly require action.

In the next chapter, you'll learn exactly what to do **when something does go wrong**—so response is structured, calm, and effective.

DECISION FRAME — UNEXPECTED SCORE DROP

Situation:

Your score drops suddenly.

Question:

Did anything new appear on your report?

□ **YES → Do this:**

- Investigate the new item
- Act only if it's unauthorized or incorrect

□ **NO → Do this:**

- Check utilization on high-impact cards
- Wait one reporting cycle
- Do nothing else

Most drops are timing-related, not threats.

CHAPTER 12
WHAT TO DO WHEN SOMETHING GOES WRONG

When something goes wrong with your credit, **how you respond matters more than how fast you panic**.

This chapter gives you a clear, time-based response plan so you always know what to do—without scrambling, overreacting, or making mistakes that slow recovery.

THE FIRST 24 HOURS: CONTAIN THE DAMAGE

The first day is about **control**, not resolution.

Your priorities:

- **Confirm the issue**

Identify exactly what changed: a new account, inquiry, balance, or personal detail.

- **Lock down access**

If your credit isn't already frozen, freeze it immediately to prevent further activity.

- **Secure accounts**

Change passwords on your primary email and any financial accounts tied to alerts.

- **Document everything**

Take screenshots, save notifications, and write down dates and details.

Do not start disputing yet.

Do not make assumptions.

Contain first—then act.

THE FIRST 7 DAYS: CORRECT AND COMMUNICATE

Once the situation is contained, you move into **correction mode**.

During this phase:

- contact the affected lender or bureau directly
- initiate the appropriate dispute or fraud report
- place fraud alerts if necessary
- follow instructions carefully and keep records

This is where accuracy beats urgency.

Clear documentation and calm communication resolve issues faster than rushed actions.

THE FIRST 30 DAYS: FOLLOW THROUGH AND STABILIZE

Most credit issues are not resolved instantly.

Over the next 30 days:

- monitor responses from bureaus and lenders
- respond promptly to requests for verification
- confirm corrections once updates post

- ensure no new unauthorized activity appears

This phase is about **closure**—making sure the issue is actually resolved, not just acknowledged.

STAYING CALM AND EFFECTIVE

Credit problems feel personal—but they're procedural.

Staying effective means:

- following a checklist instead of emotions
- focusing on facts, not fear
- trusting the process you've prepared

People who struggle the most aren't the ones with problems.

They're the ones without a plan.

You now have one.

THE ADVANTAGE OF PREPARATION

When you know what to do at each stage, problems lose their power.

You don't panic.

You don't freeze.

You respond.

In the next chapter, you'll learn how to use disputes **for protection—not repair**—so you don't create unnecessary risk while fixing real issues.

DECISION FRAME — FRAUD VS. ERROR

Situation:

Something looks wrong on your report.

Question:

Did I authorize this activity?

☐ **NO → Do this:**

- Treat as fraud
- Freeze credit
- Contact lender and bureaus

☐ **YES / UNSURE → Do this:**

- Treat as reporting error
- Document and monitor
- Dispute only if confirmed

Correct classification prevents overreaction.

CHAPTER 13
DISPUTES FOR PROTECTION (NOT REPAIR)

Disputes are powerful—but only when used **for the right reason**.

Most people associate disputes with credit repair: removing negatives, correcting old damage, or challenging past mistakes.

In this phase, your goal is different.

This chapter explains how to use disputes **defensively**, so you protect your credit without creating new risk.

DEFENSIVE VS. CORRECTIVE DISPUTES

Not all disputes serve the same purpose.

Corrective disputes are used during credit repair.

They focus on:

- fixing past errors
- correcting inaccurate negatives
- challenging outdated or incorrect information

Those disputes aim to **change history**.

Defensive disputes, on the other hand, aim to **protect the present**.

They are used when:

- a new account appears that you didn't open
- an inquiry shows up without authorization
- a balance, limit, or status is clearly incorrect
- personal information changes unexpectedly

Defensive disputes are about stopping damage—not rewriting the past.

WHEN DISPUTES HELP—AND WHEN THEY HURT

Used correctly, disputes:

- prevent unauthorized activity from spreading
- speed up corrections
- protect your score from long-term impact

Used incorrectly, they can:

- delay legitimate applications
- trigger unnecessary reviews
- complicate underwriting decisions
- make your credit profile look unstable

Disputes help when the issue is:

- new
- clearly wrong
- unauthorized
- time-sensitive

They hurt when they are:

- speculative
- emotional
- applied to accurate information
- used excessively

Protection favors **precision**, not volume.

AVOIDING UNNECESSARY RISK

One of the biggest mistakes people make is disputing *everything* out of fear.

This creates problems such as:

- accounts being flagged during lending reviews
- temporary score distortions
- delays in major financial decisions

Before disputing, ask:

- Is this new or unexpected?
- Is it clearly inaccurate or unauthorized?
- Will waiting cause more harm than action?

If the answer isn't clear, pause.

Sometimes the safest move is **monitoring**, not disputing.

THE PROTECTION RULE

Disputes are a **tool**, not a reflex.

When you use them deliberately:

- they protect progress
- they limit exposure
- they preserve stability

When used carelessly, they introduce new uncertainty.

In the next chapter, you'll learn how to maintain protection over time—**without constant monitoring or stress**—so defense becomes routine, not reaction.

DISPUTE SAFETY CHECKLIST

A decision guide that helps you:

- determine when a dispute is necessary
- avoid disputing accurate or low-risk information
- protect your score during defensive corrections

Precision over panic.

(Download in Bonus Section)

DECISION FRAME — CONSIDERING A DISPUTE

Situation:

You're thinking about filing a dispute.

Question:

Is the item new, unauthorized, or clearly wrong?

☐ **YES → Do this:**

- File a targeted defensive dispute

☐ **NO → Do this:**

- Do not dispute
- Monitor only

Disputes are scalpels, not hammers.

PART V — LONG-TERM CREDIT DEFENSE

CHAPTER 14
MONITORING WITHOUT OBSESSION

Credit protection fails when it turns into constant vigilance.

It succeeds when it becomes **routine**.

This chapter shows you how to monitor your credit in a way that is calm, efficient, and sustainable—so protection supports your life instead of dominating it.

MONTHLY AND QUARTERLY ROUTINES

Effective credit monitoring follows a rhythm.

Monthly check (10–15 minutes):

- scan for new accounts or inquiries
- confirm balances and limits still make sense
- note any unexpected changes

This is not a deep dive.

It's a scan for *new or unusual activity*.

Quarterly review (30 minutes):

- review full credit reports

- confirm personal information accuracy
- verify long-term trends in utilization and score stability

Quarterly reviews catch slow-moving issues before they matter—without pulling you into constant checking.

TOOLS VS. HABITS

Many people rely on tools and ignore habits.

Monitoring tools:

- provide alerts
- show score changes
- surface new activity

Habits:

- determine how you respond
- prevent overreaction
- maintain consistency

Tools are helpful—but they are **reactive**.

Habits are protective.

A tool without a habit creates anxiety.

A habit without a tool creates blind spots.

The goal is balance.

AVOIDING ANXIETY-DRIVEN DECISIONS

Overmonitoring creates false urgency.

Common reactions include:

- disputing harmless changes
- freezing and unfreezing unnecessarily
- second-guessing sound strategies

- making emotional decisions under stress

To avoid this:

- limit how often you check
- define clear triggers for action
- trust trends over single data points

Anxiety clouds judgment.

Structure restores it.

THE CALM ADVANTAGE

When monitoring is intentional:

- alerts inform instead of alarm
- decisions remain deliberate
- confidence replaces fear

Credit protection works best when it's boring.

If you're calm, the system is doing its job.

In the next chapter, you'll learn how major life events increase credit risk—and how to prepare for them before they happen.

MONTHLY CREDIT CHECK SHEET

A focused review sheet that helps you:

- scan for new accounts or inquiries
- confirm balances and personal information
- monitor trends without overchecking

Protection without obsession.

(Download in Bonus Section)

DECISION FRAME — HOW OFTEN TO CHECK

Situation:

You're tempted to check your credit again.

Question:

Is there a new alert or known risk?

□ **YES → Do this:**

- Review the specific issue

□ **NO → Do this:**

- Wait until your next scheduled check

Overchecking creates anxiety, not protection.

CHAPTER 15
LIFE EVENTS THAT INCREASE CREDIT RISK

Credit risk doesn't increase only because of bad decisions.

It often increases during **major life changes**—especially when your attention is focused elsewhere.

This chapter shows you how to protect your credit during transitions, when mistakes are more likely and detection is slower.

JOB CHANGES

Starting a new job, losing one, or changing income levels creates temporary instability—even if your long-term outlook is strong.

Risk increases when:

- income timing shifts
- autopay relies on an old checking account
- stress reduces attention to details

Protective actions:

- confirm all minimum payments are covered during transitions
- delay new credit applications until income stabilizes

- switch to maintenance mode if cash flow feels uncertain

Job changes aren't dangerous by default.

Unadjusted systems are.

MOVES AND ADDRESS CHANGES

Moving is one of the most overlooked credit risk events.

New addresses:

- increase the chance of misdirected mail
- create opportunities for identity confusion
- often trigger reporting inconsistencies

Protective actions:

- update addresses with lenders and bureaus promptly
- forward mail for longer than you think you need
- review reports after the move settles

Many credit issues begin with **missed communication**, not missed payments.

DIVORCE OR SEPARATION

Separation introduces both emotional and financial complexity.

Common risks include:

- joint accounts becoming unclear
- missed payments due to miscommunication
- authorized users not being removed
- assumptions about responsibility

Protective actions:

- clarify ownership of every account
- remove authorized users where appropriate

- monitor joint accounts closely until resolved

Credit doesn't understand relationship changes.

You must manage the transition intentionally.

DEATH IN THE FAMILY

Loss creates urgency, confusion, and administrative overload.

Risk increases when:

- accounts are left unattended
- access credentials are unclear
- responsibility shifts unexpectedly

Protective actions:

- identify which accounts require immediate attention
- maintain minimum payments during probate or transitions
- avoid closing accounts without understanding implications

During grief, simplicity matters.

Protection should reduce decisions—not add to them.

THE PATTERN BEHIND LIFE EVENTS

Life events don't cause credit damage.

Unadjusted systems do.

Whenever life changes, pause and ask:

- What assumptions just broke?
- Which systems need temporary support?

Preparation doesn't prevent change.

It prevents damage *because* of change.

In the next chapter, you'll learn how to keep your credit safe over time—so protection becomes part of your life, not something you remember only during crises.

DECISION FRAME — RISK SPIKE

Situation:

Your life situation changes (move, job change, divorce, loss).

Question:

Does this increase distraction or exposure?

□ **YES → Do this:**

- Tighten defenses
- Keep freeze active
- Increase monitoring temporarily

□ **NO → Do this:**

- Maintain normal routine

Protection should adapt to life, not ignore it.

CHAPTER 16
KEEPING YOUR SCORE SAFE OVER TIME

Protecting your credit isn't about one action.

It's about **maintaining conditions where damage is unlikely to happen**.

Once systems are in place, your focus shifts from defense to **stability**—keeping your score resilient over time, even as life changes.

BEHAVIORAL RULES THAT PROTECT CREDIT

Long-term protection depends more on behavior than tools.

The most effective rules are simple and repeatable:

- **Never ignore unfamiliar activity**

Small, unexplained changes deserve attention—even if they seem harmless.

- **Keep utilization intentionally low**

Low balances create buffer. Buffer absorbs mistakes.

- **Avoid reactive credit decisions**

Applications, disputes, or changes should be planned—not emotional.

- **Treat credit access as permission-based**

If access isn't needed, it stays restricted.

These rules don't require constant effort.

They remove opportunities for damage before it starts.

WHAT LONG-TERM SCORE STABILITY ACTUALLY LOOKS LIKE

A stable credit score doesn't move much—and that's a good thing.

Over time, stability shows up as:

- smaller score fluctuations
- faster recovery from minor changes
- fewer unexplained drops
- consistent reporting cycles

Stability means your profile can absorb:

- normal spending
- reporting delays
- temporary balance shifts

Without overreacting.

That resilience is what lenders trust most.

WHEN TO TIGHTEN DEFENSES

Protection should adjust with context.

Consider tightening defenses when:

- you aren't planning to apply for credit
- your score has recently improved

- your personal information exposure increases
- life events create distraction or uncertainty

Tightening defenses might mean:

- keeping freezes active longer
- increasing review frequency temporarily
- limiting credit usage further

These adjustments aren't permanent.

They're **situational safeguards**.

THE LONG VIEW

Credit protection isn't about eliminating risk.

It's about **reducing impact**.

When habits are solid and defenses adapt to your life, your score becomes difficult to disrupt—and easy to maintain.

That's the real goal:

not constant vigilance,

but **quiet, durable control**.

In the final section, we'll tie everything together—so protection becomes part of your identity, not just a phase.

DECISION FRAME — TIGHTEN OR RELAX DEFENSES

Situation:

You're reviewing your long-term protection setup.

Question:

Is my situation stable right now?

□ **YES → Do this:**

- Maintain current protection level

□ **NO → Do this:**

- Tighten defenses temporarily
- Return to normal once stable

Protection is dynamic, not permanent lockdown.

COMMON MYTHS & DANGEROUS ADVICE

This section exists to protect you—not just from fraud, but from **bad advice**.

Some of the most damaging credit mistakes don't come from criminals.

They come from **well-meaning recommendations** that sound logical, feel safe, and quietly create risk.

These myths are common.

They are repeated often.

And believing them costs people progress every single year.

MYTH 1 — "YOU DON'T NEED MONITORING SERVICES"

This statement is **half true**, which makes it dangerous.

You don't need *paid* monitoring services to protect your credit.

But you do need **awareness**.

The real mistake is thinking:

"If something goes wrong, I'll notice."

Many people don't.

Monitoring isn't about watching numbers move.

It's about **being notified when something new appears**.

Free tools + structured habits beat expensive subscriptions every time.

The danger isn't skipping services.

It's skipping systems.

MYTH 2 — "FREEZING YOUR CREDIT WILL HURT YOU"

This fear keeps millions of people exposed.

A credit freeze:

- does not hurt your score
- does not affect existing accounts
- does not prevent you from applying for credit

It only prevents **unauthorized access**.

The idea that freezing is "extreme" comes from misunderstanding—not reality.

A freeze isn't restriction.

It's **permission-based access**.

You decide when credit is available.

That's control—not damage.

MYTH 3 — "DISPUTING EVERYTHING IS PROTECTION"

This is one of the most destructive beliefs in credit protection.

Disputes are not shields.

They are **surgical tools**.

Disputing everything:

- creates unnecessary flags
- complicates underwriting decisions
- delays legitimate applications
- introduces instability into a clean profile

Protection is selective.

The safest credit profiles are not the most disputed ones.

They are the most **stable** ones.

MYTH 4 — "IF IT'S ACCURATE, IT CAN'T HURT YOU"

Accuracy doesn't equal harmless.

Even accurate information can:

- be reported at the wrong time
- be duplicated
- reappear unexpectedly
- interact poorly with improved credit

Protection isn't about erasing reality.

It's about **managing exposure and timing**.

MYTH 5 — "DOING NOTHING IS THE SAFEST OPTION"

Inaction feels safe because it avoids responsibility.

But doing nothing is still a decision.

It means:

- delays grow longer
- errors remain unchallenged
- fraud spreads quietly
- reaction replaces preparation

Protection doesn't require constant action.

But it does require **intentional safeguards**.

MYTH 6 — "IF MY CREDIT IS GOOD, I DON'T NEED PROTECTION"

This is when protection matters most.

Improved credit:

- has more value
- attracts more opportunity
- creates more exposure

High credit isn't safer.

It's more visible.

That visibility requires defense.

THE REAL DANGER ISN'T FRAUD

The real danger is **confidence without structure**.

People lose credit progress because they assume:

- "nothing will happen"
- "I'll deal with it later"
- "this advice sounds reasonable"

Protection replaces assumptions with systems.

Good credit advice should make you calmer—not busier.

If a recommendation increases fear, urgency, or obsession,

it's probably not protection.

The safest credit strategies are quiet, boring, and deliberate.

And that's exactly what this book is teaching you to build.

DECISION FRAMES — HOW TO RESPOND WITHOUT PANIC

These decision frames exist for one reason:

to remove hesitation at the exact moment it matters.

Most credit mistakes don't happen because people don't know the rules.

They happen because, in the moment, people don't know **which rule applies now**.

Decision Frames solve that.

Each frame answers one question:

"If this happens, what should I do—and what should I not do?"

BONUS SECTION — PRINTABLES & TOOLS

(ACCESSED VIA QR CODE)

This book is designed to protect your credit in real life—not just in theory.

That's why you also get a complete set of **practical printables and action tools** to help you implement everything calmly, correctly, and without guesswork.

Each tool is purpose-built to support **prevention, detection, and response**, so protection becomes a system—not a reaction.

CREDIT FREEZE CHECKLIST

A clear, step-by-step checklist to:

- freeze your credit correctly at all bureaus
- confirm protection is fully active
- avoid common setup mistakes

This ensures your strongest defense is in place—and stays there.

A calm, time-based action plan for:

- the first 24 hours
- the first 7 days
- the first 30 days

So if something ever goes wrong, you're not scrambling—you're executing.

MONTHLY CREDIT CHECK SHEET

A focused review sheet that helps you:

- scan for new accounts or inquiries
- confirm balances and personal information
- monitor trends without overchecking

Protection without obsession.

DISPUTE SAFETY CHECKLIST

A decision guide that helps you:

- determine when a dispute is necessary
- avoid disputing accurate or low-risk information
- protect your score during defensive corrections

Precision over panic.

EMERGENCY CREDIT LOCK GUIDE

A quick-reference guide for moments when risk spikes:

- travel
- major life events
- suspected exposure

It shows you how to temporarily tighten defenses—then safely return to normal.

HOW TO ACCESS YOUR TOOLS

Scan the QR code included in this book to access and download all printable worksheets and tools.

Use them as needed—not all at once.

They're here to support you, not overwhelm you.

Together, these tools turn **Credit Protection Blueprint** into a complete defense system—one that protects your progress quietly, consistently, and for the long term.

FINAL MESSAGE

PROTECTION IS WHAT TURNS PROGRESS INTO PERMANENCE

If there's one truth to carry forward from this book, it's this:

You didn't lose credit in the past because you were careless.

You lost it because it wasn't protected.

Once credit improves, the rules change.

The goal is no longer repair or acceleration—it's **preservation**.

And preservation doesn't require fear.

It requires systems.

CONFIDENCE WITHOUT PARANOIA

Real credit protection feels calm.

It doesn't mean:

- checking your credit every day

- reacting to every notification
- living in constant alert mode

It means knowing:

- access is controlled
- early warnings won't be missed
- responses are already planned

When systems are in place, anxiety disappears—and confidence takes its place.

YOUR CLEAR NEXT STEPS

From here, keep it simple:

1. Keep your **credit freeze active** when you don't need access
2. Follow your **monthly check routine**, not daily monitoring
3. Use checklists when something changes—don't improvise
4. Tighten defenses during life events or uncertainty
5. Return to normal mode once stability is restored

Protection works best when it's **boring and repeatable**.

COMPLETE THE BLUEPRINT

Each book in this series has a role:

- **Credit Repair Blueprint** — fix what was broken
- **Debt Payoff Blueprint** — take control and reduce pressure
- **Credit Protection Blueprint** — protect what you rebuilt

Progress creates opportunity.

Protection preserves it.

Completing the trilogy turns short-term wins into long-term stability.

ONE LAST REMINDER

You don't need to eliminate risk.

You need to **control exposure**.

You now have the blueprint.

Use it—and keep what you built.

www.ingramcontent.com/pod-product-compliance
Lightning Source LLC
LaVergne TN
LVHW082356200926
848481LV00012B/3586